A New Tune A for Drums

The Drum edition of *A New Tune A Day* is designed to be partly compatible with the Electric Guitar and Bass Guitar editions.

From lesson 9, each lesson contains at least one piece common to all three books, indicated by the symbols:

Look for these symbols within the book.

Boston Music Company
part of The Music Sales Group
London/New York/Paris/Sydney/Copenhagen/Berlin/Madrid/Tokyo

CW00536856

Foreword

Since its appearance in the early 1930s, C. Paul Herfurth's original *A Tune A Day* series has become the most popular instrumental teaching method of all time. Countless music students have been set on their path by the clear, familiar, proven material, and the logical, sensibly-paced progression through the lessons within the book.

The teacher will find that the new books have been meticulously rewritten by experienced teachers: instrumental techniques and practices have been updated and the musical content has been completely overhauled.

The student will find clearly presented, uncluttered material, with familiar pieces and a gentle introduction to the theoretical aspects of music. The books are now accompanied by audio CDs of examples and backing tracks to help the student develop a sense of rhythm and performance at an early stage.

As in the original books, tests are given following every five lessons. Teachers are encouraged to present these as an opportunity to ensure that the student has a good overview of the information studied up to this point.

The following extract from the foreword to the original edition remains as true today as the day it was written:

The value of learning to count aloud from the very beginning cannot be over-estimated. Only in this way can a pupil sense rhythm. Rhythm, one of the most essential elements of music, and usually conspicuous by its absence in amateur ensemble playing, is emphasised throughout.

Eventual success in mastering the instrument depends on regular and careful application to its technical demands. Daily practice should not extend beyond the limits of the player's physical endurance – the aim should be the gradual development of control.

Music-making is a lifelong pleasure, and at its heart is a solid understanding of the principles of sound production and music theory. These books are designed to accompany the student on these crucial first steps: the rewards for study and practice are immediate and lasting. Welcome to the world of music!

Contents

Published by
Boston Music Company

Exclusive Distributors:
Music Sales Limited
14-15 Berners Street, London W1T 3LJ, UK.

Music Sales Corporation
257 Park Avenue South, New York, NY 10010, USA.

Music Sales Pty Limited
120 Rothschild Avenue, Rosebery, NSW 2018, Australia.

This book © 2008 Boston Music Company,
a division of Music Sales Limited.

Edited by David Harrison
Music processed by Paul Ewers Music Design
Original compositions and arrangements by Chris Baker
Cover and book designed by Chloë Alexander
Photography by Matthew Ward
Models: Josh Bain and Ben Romans-Hopcraft
Printed in the EU
Backing tracks by Guy Dagul
CD performance by Chris Baker, Pete Kershaw and Steve Kershaw
CD mixed and mastered by Jonas Persson and John Rose

Thanks to Graveney School, Tooting, London.

Your Guarantee of Quality

As publishers, we strive to produce every book to the highest commercial
standards. The music has been freshly engraved and the book has been
carefully designed to minimise awkward page turns and to make playing
from it a real pleasure. Throughout, the printing and binding have been
planned to ensure a sturdy, attractive publication which should give years
of enjoyment. If your copy fails to meet our high standards, please inform
us and we will gladly replace it.

www.musicsales.com

Rhythm basics

The stave

Drum music is written on a grid of five lines called a *stave*.
At the beginning of each stave is placed a special symbol called a *clef*.

This example shows a drum clef, generally used for untuned percussion instruments.

The stave is divided into equal sections of time, called bars or measures, by barlines.

Note values

Different symbols are used to show the time value of *notes*, and each *note value* has an equivalent symbol for a rest, representing silence.

The **quaver** (or *eighth note*), often used to signify a half beat, is written with a solid head and a stem with a tail. The quaver rest is also shown.

The **crotchet** (or *quarter note*), often used to signify one beat, is written with a solid head and a stem. The crotchet rest is also shown.

The **minim** (or *half note*) is worth two crotchets. It is written with a hollow head and a stem. The minim rest is placed on the middle line.

The **semibreve** (or *whole note*) is worth two minims. It is written with a hollow head. The semibreve rest hangs from the fourth line.

Other note values

Note values can be increased by half by adding a dot after the note head. Here a minim and a crotchet are together worth a *dotted* minim.

Grouping quavers

Where two or more quavers follow each other, they can be joined by a *beam* from stem to stem.

Time signatures

The number of beats in a bar is determined by the *time signature*, a pair of numbers placed after the clef.

The upper number shows how many beats each bar contains, whilst the lower number indicates what kind of note value is used to represent a single beat.

This lower number is a fraction of a semibreve so that 4 represents crotchets and 8 represents quavers.

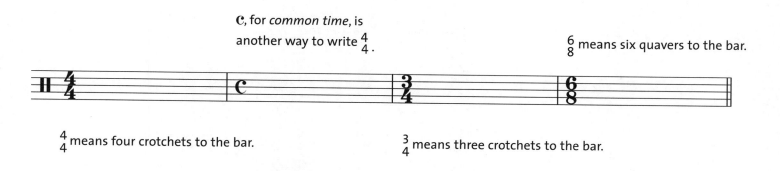

C, for *common time*, is another way to write $\frac{4}{4}$.

$\frac{6}{8}$ means six quavers to the bar.

$\frac{4}{4}$ means four crotchets to the bar.

$\frac{3}{4}$ means three crotchets to the bar.

Drum notation

Different elements of the drum kit are represented by symbols placed on the stave.

This book uses the notation approved by the Percussive Arts Society (PAS).

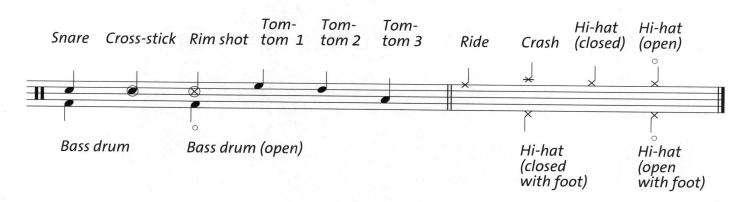

Snare   Cross-stick   Rim shot   Tom-tom 1   Tom-tom 2   Tom-tom 3   Ride   Crash   Hi-hat (closed)   Hi-hat (open)

Bass drum   Bass drum (open)   Hi-hat (closed with foot)   Hi-hat (open with foot)

Bar lines

Various different types of bar lines are used:

Double bar lines divide one section of music from another.

Final bar lines show the end of a piece of music.

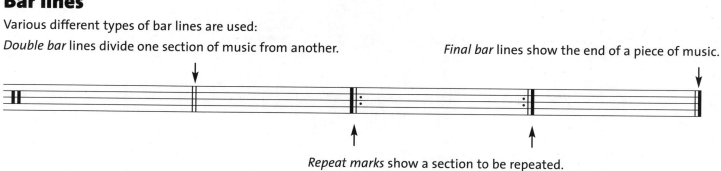

Repeat marks show a section to be repeated.

The drum kit

- Ride cymbal
- Crash cymbal
- High tom-tom
- Mid tom-tom
- Hi-hat
- Floor tom-tom
- Snare drum
- Hi-hat pedal
- Stool or throne
- Bass drum pedal
- Bass drum

- Boom
- Cymbal stand
- Tom-tom holder
- Tom-tom arm
- Bass drum spur
- Bass drum hoop

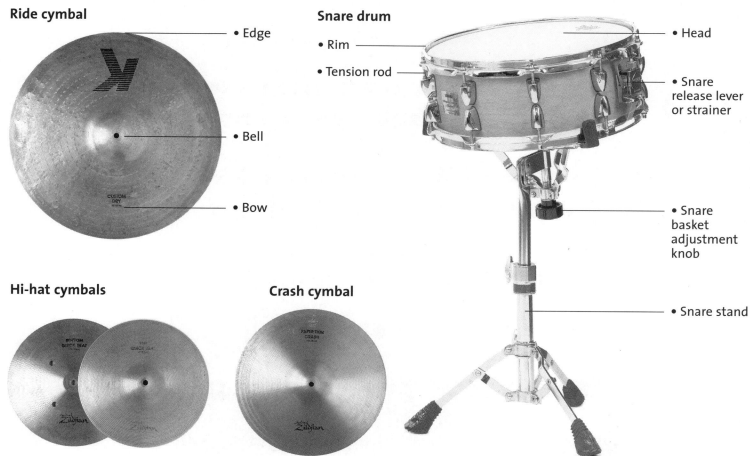

Ride cymbal
- Edge
- Bell
- Bow

Snare drum
- Rim
- Tension rod
- Head
- Snare release lever or strainer
- Snare basket adjustment knob
- Snare stand

Hi-hat cymbals

Crash cymbal

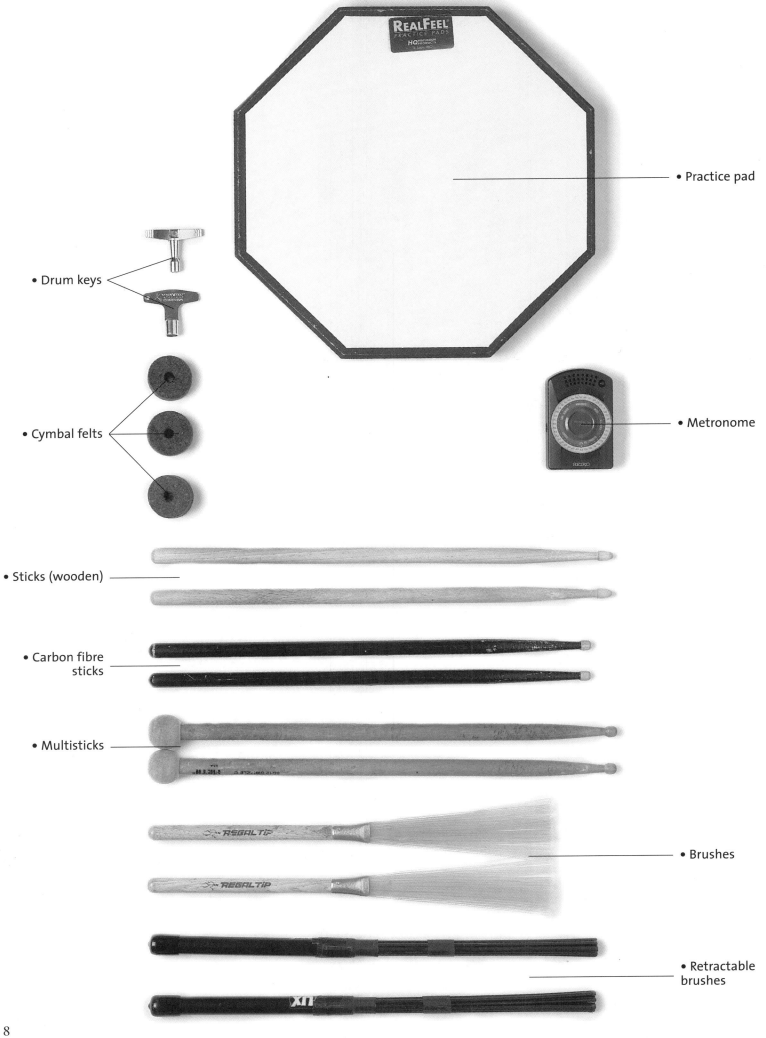

- Practice pad

- Drum keys

- Metronome

- Cymbal felts

- Sticks (wooden)

- Carbon fibre sticks

- Multisticks

- Brushes

- Retractable brushes

Posture

Set your stool at a comfortable height, making sure to keep your back straight and not to hunch your shoulders. You should be able to reach all parts of the drum kit without stretching. A good posture is essential to avoid discomfort in the shoulders, neck and back. Experiment with different stool positions and heights until you are happy.

Grip

Drum kit technique evolved through military snare playing, and the *traditional* grip is still used to some extent, whereas many players prefer the *matched* grip. In either case the standard grip requires the stick to be held at the fulcrum – the pivot point.

1 Balance the stick between thumb and forefinger, moving along the stick until you find the fulcrum.

2 Now fold the fingers under to support the stick lightly.

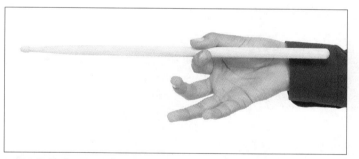

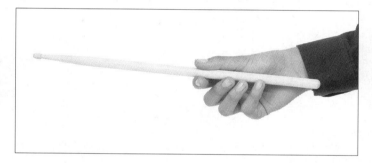

Matched grip

Here the grip is identical for both hands.

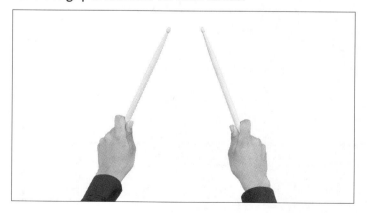

Traditional grip

Your teacher will be able to discuss the various advantages of the two types of grip, and help you decide which one to use. Many players switch between one and the other depending on particular technique and styles.

In traditional grip, the left hand is turned upward, with the stick passing between the middle and ring fingers. Again, experiment with the grip until you have found the fulcrum.

goals:

1. **Warm-ups**
2. **Accents**
3. **Rudiment 1: Single Stroke Roll**
4. **Repeat bar lines**
5. **Count and play**

Rudiments and preliminary exercises

Left-handed players should remember to reverse all sticking combinations in this book.

A *rudiment* is a basic pattern used in drumming. Rudiments are designed to develop control, strength and co-ordination. These patterns form the basic building blocks of drumming, and can be combined in any number of ways.

Rudiments should be practised on various playing surfaces, such as a practice pad, pillows, a snare drum and on the drum kit. Drummers who are familiar with the rudiments of drumming apply them to the drum kit to create their own warm-ups, patterns, fills and solos. For now, play the rudiments on the snare drum.

Preliminary exercises

Notice the repeat bar lines

‖: :‖

Whenever they appear, the music between them is played twice.

Exercise 1: Rebound Eights

Focus on the correct grip: start with the fulcrum grip ...

... then add fingers with relaxed arms with elbows and shoulders down.

Play eight strokes with each hand

Allow the sticks to bounce back up to the same height.

Exercise 2: Double Trouble

Play double strokes with each hand on beats one and three for two bars.

This is an excellent exercise for creating clear double strokes. Make sure that the second beat of each double stroke is the same volume as the first.

Exercise 3: One-To-Eights

The drum kit requires both mental and physical control. It is important that the muscles are warm. This exercise is a great warm-up.

Play a single stroke with each hand, then two with each, then three, building up to eight with each hand. Try this slowly at first, then take a short rest and play again a little faster. Notice how your reflexes improve as you warm up.

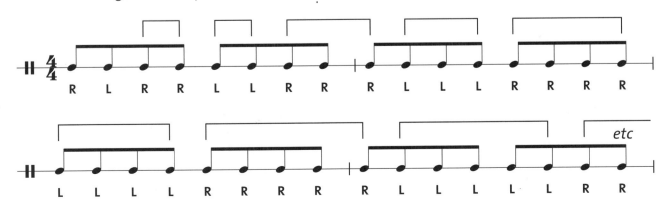

etc

Accents

To emphasise a note, an accent $>$ is used: try playing the previous exercise, but this time play the accented notes a little louder than the others.

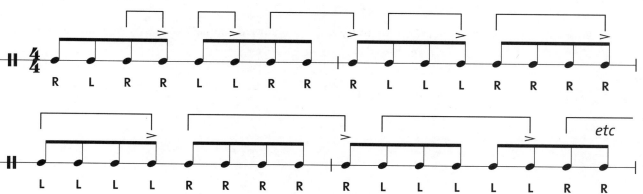

Remember to play with a metronome. Focus on staying as relaxed as possible, and maintain an even bounce with each hand.

Exercise 4: single stroke roll preparation

This exercise prepares for the Single Stroke Roll.

Play at a steady tempo, and try to make the strokes sound as alike as possible.

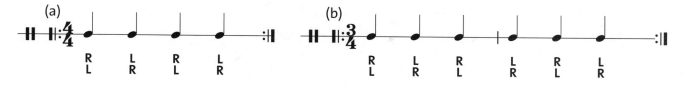

Rudiment 1: The Single Stroke Roll

This rudiment consists of single alternate strokes with each hand performed at speed. In order to build up speed, work through these exercises steadily:

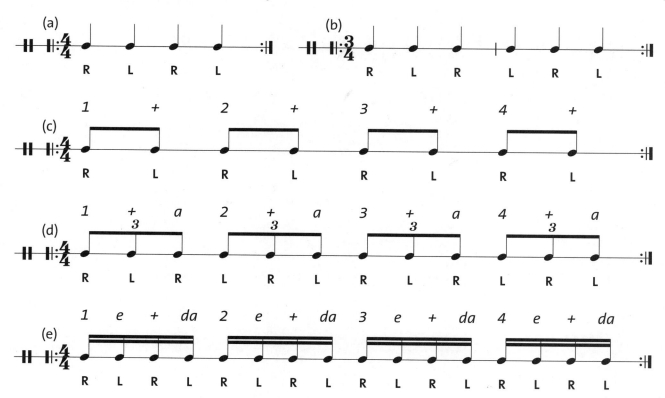

Sight-reading exercises:

Practise slowly, and with a metronome. Try playing them with your teacher at various tempos. Ask your teacher to play these exercises while you play just the rests.

The practice tracks on the CD are a great way to try out the rudiments and other exercises as you learn them.

(a)

(b)

(c)

(d)

Piece for Lesson 1

Au Clair de la Lune — French traditional

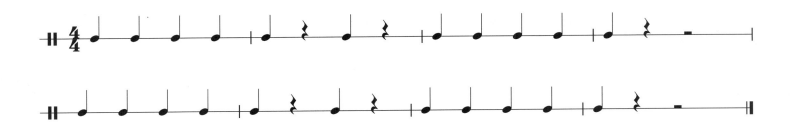

Rudiment 2: The Single Paradiddle

Para signifies two strokes with alternate hands, while the *diddle* describes two strokes with same hand.

So the sticking pattern for a single paradiddle is **R L R R** or **L R L L**

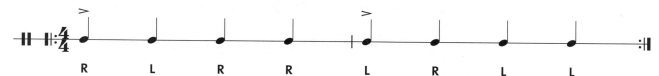

Now try the single paradiddle in quavers and then in semiquavers.

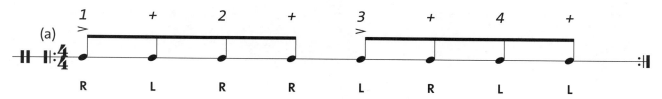

When this becomes natural, try accenting the paradiddle differently:

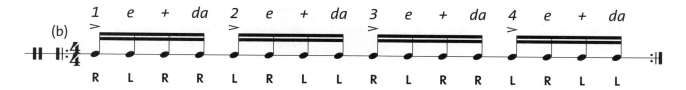

You could also try beginning a paradiddle at a different point:

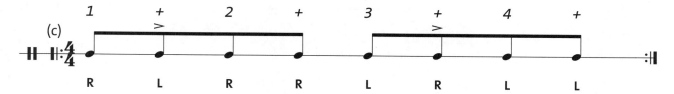

As you play faster, notice how the second note of the 'diddle' is played using the natural bounce of the stick on the drumhead. Don't forget to play both notes at the same volume.

All these exercises should be played 'right hand lead' (start the pattern with the right hand each time) or 'alternate sticking' (play the pattern starting from the right, then play it starting from the left, etc).

Lesson 2

Sight-reading exercises:

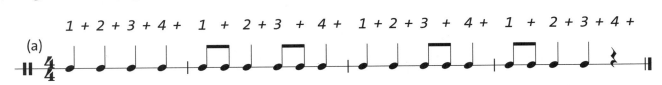

(a)

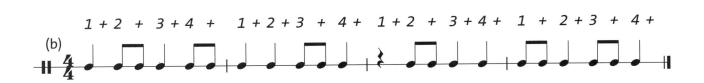

(b)

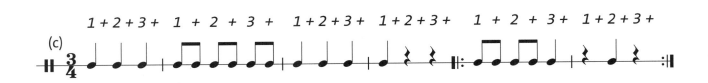

(c)

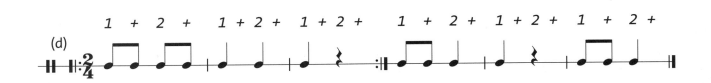

(d)

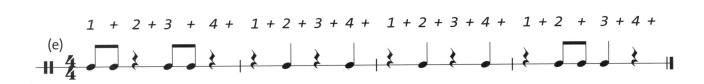

(e)

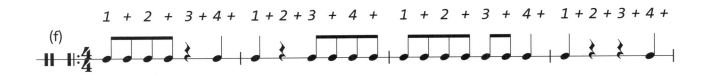

(f)

Duets:

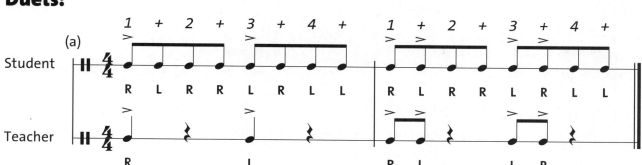

Piece for Lesson 2

Twinkle Twinkle, Little Star

Traditional

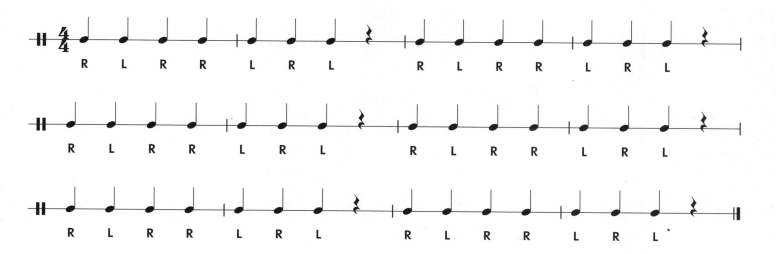

Lesson 3 goals:

1. **Rudiment 3: Double Paradiddle**
2. **Rudiment 4: Flam**
3. **Grace notes**
4. **Rudiment 5: Single Flam Paradiddle**

Rudiment 3: The Double Paradiddle

The Double Paradiddle could be thought of as a 'para-para-diddle', with two pairs of alternating strokes followed by a double stroke. Notice that (b) is in $\frac{6}{8}$.

This time signature is built of two beats, each divisible into three quavers. A paradiddle can equally easily be practised in $\frac{3}{4}$ or $\frac{6}{8}$.

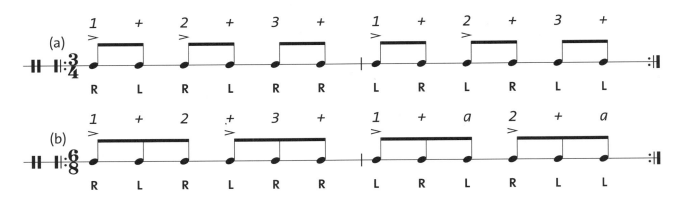

Rudiment 4: The Flam

The *Flam* is an accented note preceded by a *grace* note.

The notes are played as close together as possible, creating a 'thicker' main note:

A grace note is a short embellishment played just before a main note, and shown as a small quaver: with a line through the tail it should be played as quickly as possible.

The grace note should be played from about two inches above the drumhead, with the main note played from eight to ten inches above the head.

Try this with left hand lead, and then with right hand lead. Practise very slowly at first, being aware of quality and consistency of each flam.

Rudiment 5: The Single Flam Paradiddle

Flams and paradiddles can be attached together to create a flam paradiddle:

Try this slowly at first, and build up steadily to a brisk tempo.

Now play these exercises with your teacher. Aim for crisp, accurate flams.

When you feel confident, swap parts and play the flam paradiddles

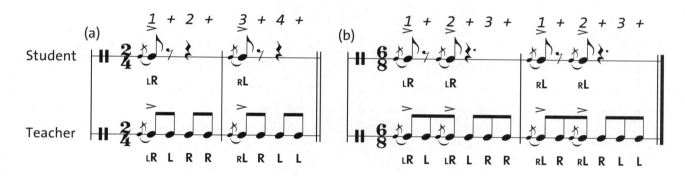

Sight-reading exercises:

Lesson 3

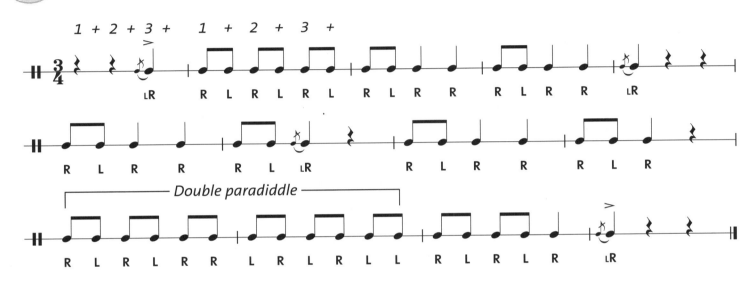

PRACTICE ROUTINES

Practise at all tempos and track your progress by keeping a notebook record of metronome settings and dates at which you can perform all of your rudimental and reading exercises.

Piece for Lesson 3

6–7

Anitra's Dance

Edvard Grieg

1. **Rudiment 6: Double Stroke Roll**
2. **Tempo transition**
3. **Repeat last bar symbol**

Rudiment 6: The Double Stroke Roll

Also known as the *long roll*, this rudiment comprises a sequence of two consecutive strokes played with each hand. Each stroke should be performed with equal volume. Try the following:

When you start to play this exercise at speed you will notice that the second stroke moves from being played with the wrist to a finger stroke that is bounced off the playing surface. Make sure that the second stroke is as clear as the first.

Exercise 1: Mind The Gap

Play and count aloud together. Swap hands, and then combine the two parts for a double stroke roll.

Try starting slowly and very deliberately, gradually increasing the tempo before returning to the original speed – see how fast you can go without losing control!

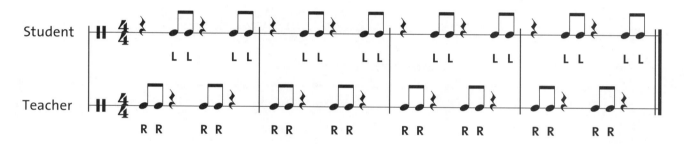

CONTROL TECHNIQUES

Notice how the focus of control for the double stroke changes from the elbow (at very slow speeds), through the wrist as you get faster, until it becomes a more intuitive finger movement when the roll is in full flow.

'Repeat last bar' symbol

To save space, and to make music easier to read, this symbol ⦸ is often used to denote that the bar in question contains exactly the same music as the previous bar.

Two bars repeated can be shown with this symbol ⦸.

Look out for the ⦸ in the following exercise.

Sight-reading exercises:

(a)
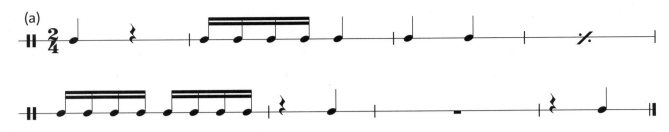

(b)
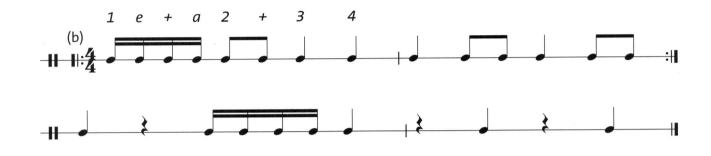

(c)

(d)

(e)

Piece for Lesson 4

Early One Morning

English traditional

1. **Rudiment 7: Flam Tap**
2. **Rudiment 8: Flam Accent**
3. **Dynamics**

Rudiment 7: The Flam Tap

The *Flam Tap* is essentially a flam followed by an unaccented note.

Try these:

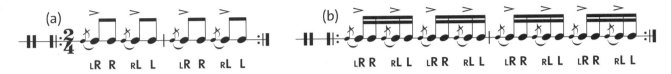

(a) LR R RL L LR R RL L

(b) LR R RL L LR R RL L LR R RL L LR R RL L

Rudiment 8: The Flam Accent

The *Flam Accent* is a flam followed by two unaccented notes. The following exercises outline some of the rhythmic variations possible with the flam accent:

(a) LR L R RL R L LR L R RL R L

(b) LR L R RL R L LR L R RL R L

(c) LR L R RL R L LR L R RL R L

(d) LR L R RL R L LR L R RL R L

The exercises on this page are great for building technique and co-ordination.

DYNAMICS

Music uses Italian words to describe how loudly or quietly to play.
These words or abbreviations are called 'Dynamic Markings'.

Forte (written as f) = **loud**   *Piano* (written as p) = **quiet**

The following symbols are used when gradually changing dynamics:

Crescendo (often written as cresc.) = gradually louder. Also shown by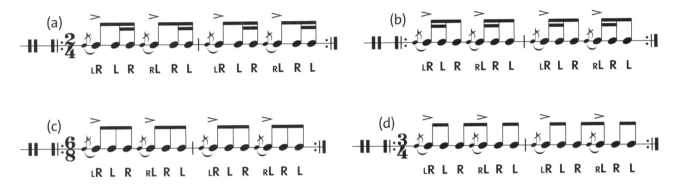

Diminuendo (often written as dim.) = gradually quieter. Also shown by

A dynamic marking especially useful for drummers is *sforzando*, indicating
a strong, sudden accent. This is usually shown as sf or sfz

Sight-reading exercises:

(a)

(b)

(c)
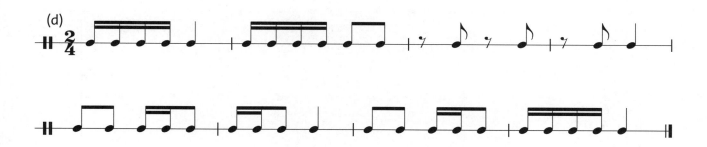

(d)

(e)

Exercise 1: Flam-tastic

Piece for Lesson 5

10-11

The First Nowell

Traditional

Flam accents

Flam accents

24

test:

for Lessons 1 to 5

1. Name that part

Correctly name every drum in your kit

(10)

2. Sign language

Draw the following:

- repeat marks
- accent
- crotchet rest
- crescendo

- two quavers joined together

(10)

3. Notation

Write and play a paradiddle:

(10)

4. Bar-lines

Fill in the bar-lines for a piece in 4/4:

(10)

5. Rudiments

Play the following rudiments:

- Double Stroke Roll
- Flam
- Flam Tap

- Single Flam Paradiddle
- Double Paradiddle

(10)

Total (50)

1. **Measuring tempo**
2. **Rudiment 9: The Drag**
3. **Rudiment 10: Five-Stroke Roll**

MEASURING TEMPO

The tempo of a piece of music is the speed of the underlying pulse, or beat.

It is measured in beats per minute, and this measurement is indicated at the beginning of a piece of music.

This example shows that the beats are displayed in crotchets, and that there are 120 of them per minute. ♩ = 120

When the indicated tempo is too fast to be counted in crotchets, a minim is used. ♩ = 100

Italian terms are also used to show the tempo.
Here are a few of the most common ones:

Presto = Very Fast   **Andante** = At Walking Pace
Allegro = Fast   **Adagio** = Slowly
Moderato = Moderately   **Lento** = Very Slowly

In ensemble playing, drummers are often responsible for maintaining the correct tempo.

Try to develop a sense of different tempos and practise keeping them steady.

Rudiment 9: The Drag

The *Drag* is similar to a flam, but with two grace notes preceding the main note:

Try to position your sticks as you would for a flam, with the grace notes played from a height of two inches, and the main note played from eight to ten inches high.

```
L L R    R R L    L L R    R R L    L L R    R R L    L L R    R R L
```

You may also see the drag written as follows.

The two grace notes are abbreviated as a stroke through the stem of a standard quaver to make semiquavers:

Groups of quavers and semiquavers can be abbreviated as follows:

You'll learn more about this in lesson 7.

Rudiment 10: The Five-Stroke Roll

Try this little exercise to prepare you for the next rudiment:

Be sure to practise the five-stroke roll with left hand lead and right hand lead.

The *Five-Stroke Roll* consists of two pairs of double strokes followed by a single stroke:

You might see an abbreviated version of this rudiment as follows:

Call And Response

In music a call and response is a succession of two distinct phrases usually played by different musicians, where the second phrase is heard as a direct reply to the first.

Notice the bracketed note in bar 8: click the sticks together in the air on this note.
Swap the parts, and try playing the piece at different tempos. Be sure not to speed up in bar 7.

Sight-reading exercises:

Piece for Lesson 6

13-14   *Frère Jacques*   French traditional

1. **Alternative notation**
2. **Rudiment 11: The Buzz Roll**
3. **More dynamics**
4. **Dotted notes**

Alternative notation

Because drum notation often involves repeated notes and symbols, certain common repetitions are written in shorthand.

Four semiquavers together, for example, can also be written as a crotchet with two strokes across the stem, as shown in lesson 6:

In addition, a roll is generally notated like this:

Strictly speaking, the four strokes over the semibreve indicate that the note should be split into 64, but in practice this is taken to mean that the roll should consist of very rapid notes.

Rudiment 11: The Buzz Roll

The *Buzz Roll* is created by limiting stick bounce. Allow the stick to bounce freely at first, until it naturally comes to rest. Now try tightening the grip a little, reducing the 'give', so the stick comes back on to the drum head more rapidly.

Experiment until the stick 'buzzes' onto the head. Eventually you can alternate and overlap the buzzes until a continuous, smooth sound is achieved. The buzz roll is also known as the *press* roll: imagine *pressing* the sticks into the playing surface.

The buzz roll is shown like this:

STICK BUZZ

The length of the stick buzz is determined by:

- stick velocity (the initial 'attack' of the roll)

- pressure applied to the fulcrum (by control of the 'give' in the grip)

- drum head tension (affects the 'bounce')

Try the following exercises to help you think about fulcrum pressure adjustment:

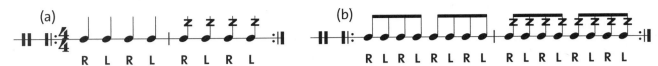

Now start softly, getting gradually louder before dying away again.

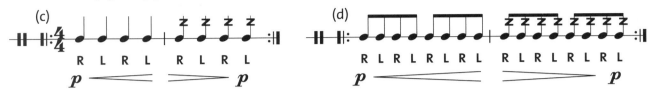

Finally, try this with semiquavers. When you've mastered this, you'll be well on your way to perfecting the buzz roll.

MORE DYNAMICS

mp = mezzo piano, meaning moderately quiet   *mf* = mezzo forte, meaning moderately loud
(mezzo literally means 'half')
pp = pianissimo, meaning very quiet   *ff* = fortissimo, meaning very loud

Duet: Rollin', Rollin', Rollin'

This duet features plenty of buzz rolls and the odd flam. Keep it steady, and aim to make the buzzes as constant as you can. Notice the importance of fulcrum control when applying buzzes and single strokes.

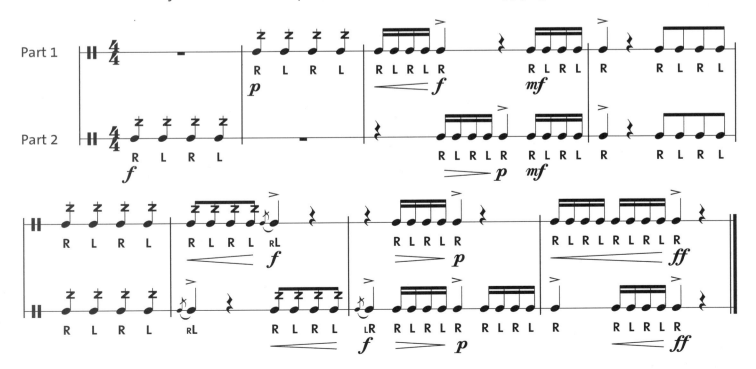

DOTTED NOTES

A dot just following a note increases its length by half. Take a look at these examples:

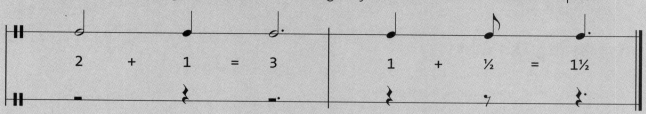

Sight-reading exercises:

Piece for Lesson 7

The Drunken Sailor

Traditional British Sea Shanty

15-16

Notice the five-stroke rolls and the flams in this piece. Keep it crisp!

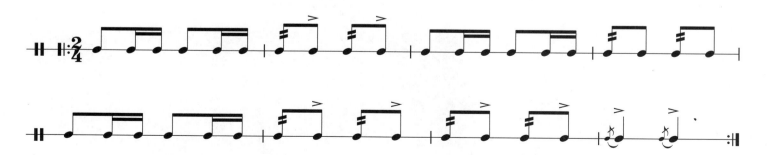

Introducing the feet

There are various techniques for playing the hi-hat and bass drum with pedals.
Below are three of the most widely-used options.

---

1. Flat-footed

a Both feet lay flat on the hi-hat and bass drum pedals. The hi-hat cymbals are at their furthest apart, and the bass drum beater is at its furthest point from the head.

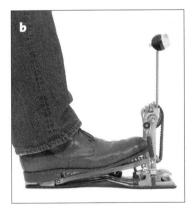

b To strike the cymbal or drum, downward pressure is applied with the full foot 'flat' of the pedal and released whilst still maintaining contact with the pedal footplate.

2. Toe technique/heel up

a The toes make contact with the pedal, and the heel is raised.

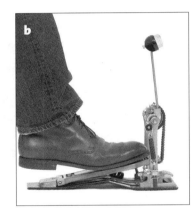

b Pressure is applied by lifting the thigh and bouncing on the pedal with the ball of the foot. This technique is used by players who require extra speed and volume.

---

3. Heel & toe/rocking motion

This technique is often used in combination with the others on the hi-hat pedal.
The foot is 'rocked' forwards and backwards in time to the music, just as you might tap your foot to a rhythm when playing any instrument.

a The toes rock forward with the heel raised, and the cymbals strike.

b The foot rocks backward onto the heel with the toes raised.

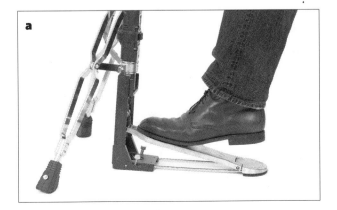

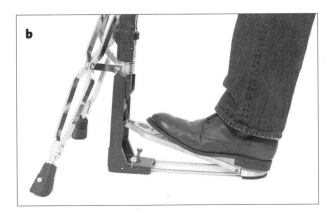

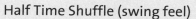

Half Time Shuffle (swing feel)

Jazz Ride Pattern (swing feel)

Reggae: The One Drop (swing feel)

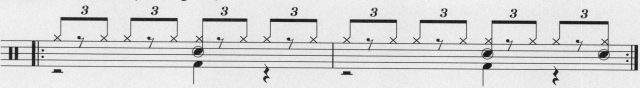

Bossa Nova

Cha Cha Cha

Son Clave 3-2

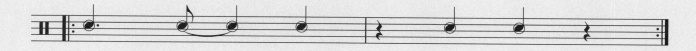

Son Clave 2-3

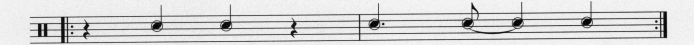

Mambo 3-2

Mambo 2-3

Bolero

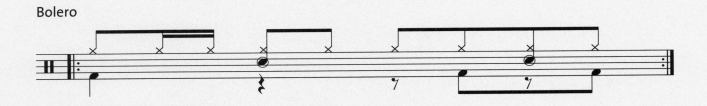

Gospel: 2 Beat Cross Stick Groove (swing feel)

New Orleans Second Line Groove (swing feel)

Motown Groove

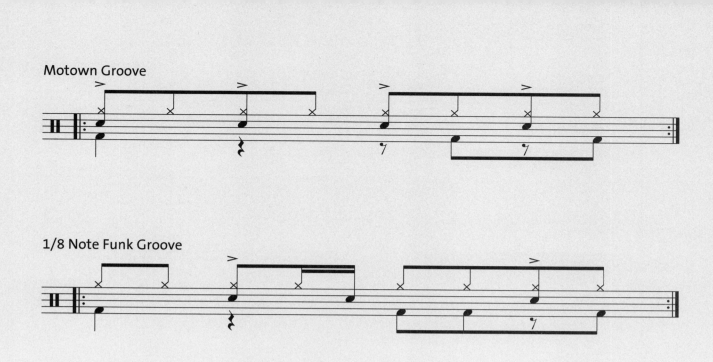

1/8 Note Funk Groove

1/16 Note Funk Groove

Hip-Hop Groove (swing feel)

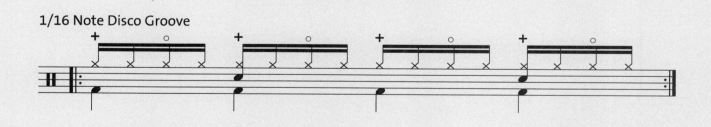

1/16 Note Disco Groove

1/8 Note Disco Groove

1/4 Note Groove

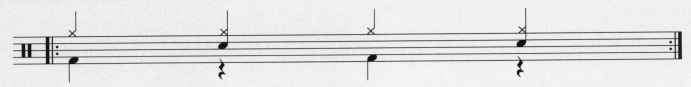

1/8 Note Groove

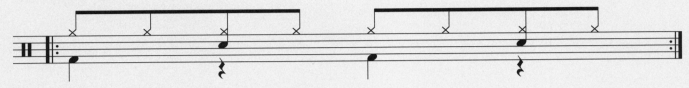

1/16 Note Groove (1 hand on the Hi Hat)

1/16 Note Groove (2 hands on the Hi Hat)

12/8 Blues

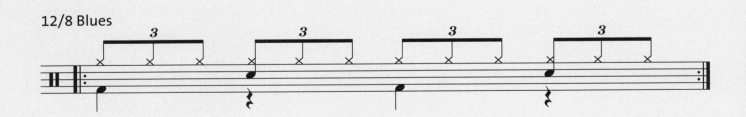

Blues Shuffle (swing feel)

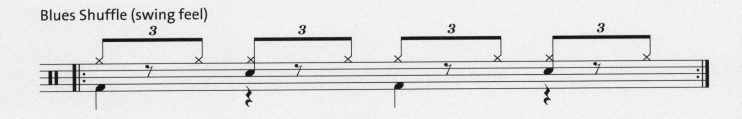

Pedal notation

Good foot technique is an essential foundation for drum kit playing, and foot exercises are great for developing control, speed and endurance.

Up till now, the music in these lessons has all been played on the snare drum, so all the notation has been on a single line. Now, as other parts of the kit are added, the music is on standard 5-line staves.

Take a look at the notation for the bass drum and hi-hat:

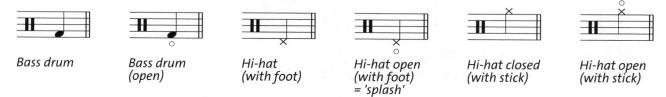

Bass drum   Bass drum (open)   Hi-hat (with foot)   Hi-hat open (with foot) = 'splash'   Hi-hat closed (with stick)   Hi-hat open (with stick)

The bass drum is played 'open' when the pedal is released on contact, allowing the drum head to reverberate. The hi-hat 'splash' is played by releasing the pedal and allowing the cymbals to ring on, loosely touching each other. Now try these exercises:

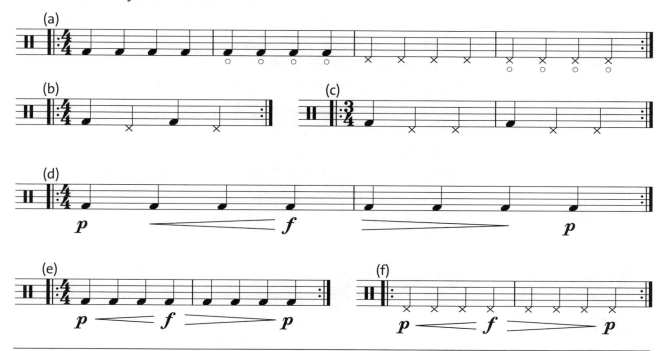

Ensure that the finish position for the bass drum is off the head for a full 'open' sound where indicated.

Triplets

A triplet is a group of three notes of the same length, and can be used to split a beat into three even if it usually splits into two:

Finally, try playing these basic rhythms with accents at the end of the beat:

Lesson 8

Ties

Sometimes, notes are extended by the use of linking lines called *ties*.

In $\frac{6}{8}$ the underlying beat is in dotted crotchets. For this reason, the tied note in the last bar is made of two tied quavers rather than a single crotchet.

This is especially useful when a note extends over a bar-line, or when the time signature requires it.

Sight-reading exercise: Big Six

Keep an eye out for the various rudiments in this exercise.

If you like, speak the names of them out loud, in time with the music!

17

RL LR RL R L R R L L R L R R L L

R L R R L L R L R R L L R L R R L R

R L R

Piece for Lesson 8

18-19

Jingle Bells

Traditional

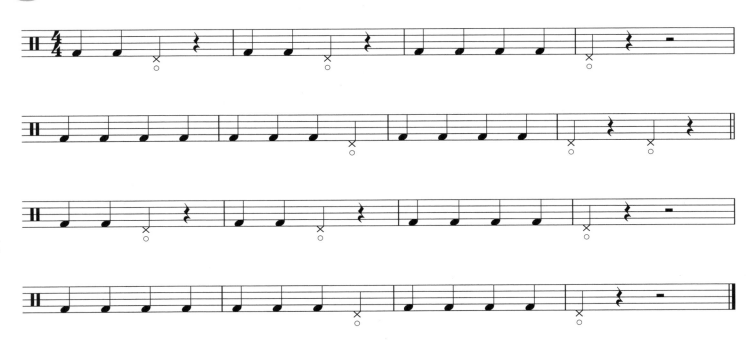

34

goals:

1. **Rock patterns**
2. **Coordination**

3. **Fills**
4. **1st and 2nd time bars**

Rock drumming

Rock music grew out of the Rock & Roll of the 1950s which in turn has its roots in the rhythm & blues style of the 1930s and '40s. For the drummer, the music is characterised by a heavy, steady *groove* (rhythm pattern) with *straight* (precise) quavers.

In rock music the main pulse is stated with the bass and snare drums. They should be prominent and played with authority. The snare drum often plays on 2 and 4, providing a *backbeat*.

Try to maintain a relaxed posture and consistent grip while performing the following exercises. This should help your *coordination* – bringing all the different parts of the rhythm together in one fluid pattern.

Photo courtesy of LFI

Keith Moon – a great innovator of rock drumming. With The Who in the 1960s, Moon developed an eccentric style, playing drums as a lead instrument, with fluid rolls and embellishments at a time when drummers were expected to play simple backbeat rhythms (see left).

Exercise 1:

Play straight quavers on the hi-hat (**a**); then add a backbeat on the snare drum (**b**); and finally play the bass drum on 1 and 3 (**c**).

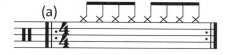  

Exercise 2:

Now experiment with different placements for the bass drum, and – in the third example (**c**) – open the hi-hat for the final quaver, returning to a closed position for the repeat.

The above exercises can also be played with the hi-hat half-open, creating a crashy sound.

The symbol for the half-open hi-hat is this:

Hi-hat half-open (with stick)

Lesson 9

Fills

A *fill* is a short rhythmic phrase inserted into a standard time-keeping pattern.
It is often used to emphasise the transition between two separate music sections, such as the verse and chorus of a song.

Fills ideas can be constructed from rolls or other drum rudiments.

Some two-beat fills:

Some four-beat fills:

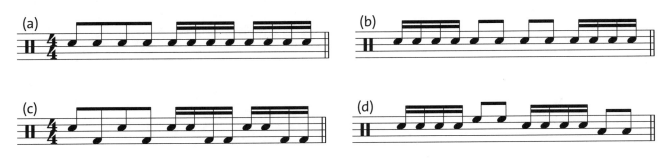

Some two-beat fills incorporating rudiments:

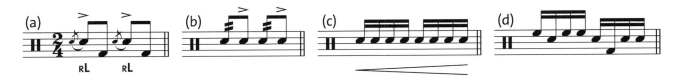

Some four-beat fills incorporating rudiments:

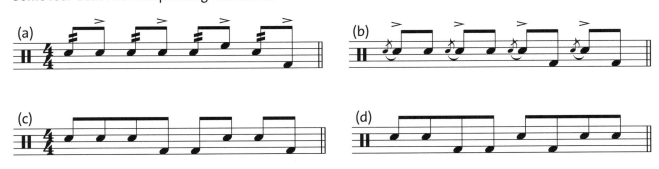

1ST AND 2ND TIME BARS

In *Auld Lang Syne* you will find signs for first and second time bars.
Play up to the repeat sign including the first time bar, then go back to the 'start repeat' sign.
On the second time through, miss out the first time ending and play the
second time ending instead.

The following piece brings together all your rock skills, and you can finally
let loose on the crash cymbal!
Play a half-open hi-hat in bar 9, and continue through the rest of the section the
same way (indicated by *sim.* – short for *simile* – meaning 'the same').
Notice that the fill is slightly different the second time through, as shown.

Piece for Lesson 9

Auld Lang Syne 🎵 🎵

Scottish traditional

goals:

1. **Blues drumming**
2. **Swing**
3. **Pattern building**
4. **Half-time feel**
5. **Pick-ups**

Mitch Mitchell – best known for his work as drummer with The Jimi Hendrix Experience, Mitchell's fluid style provided the perfect canvas for Hendrix's extended improvisations.

Photo courtesy of LFI

Blues drumming

The blues is a folk music derived from African-American spirituals and work songs popular in the early 1900s. Many traditional blues songs follow a 12-bar structure, and use a rhythm pattern called a *shuffle*, which is based on a triplet feel.

Swing

In blues, as with rock, the bass drum is prominent, with a snare drum backbeat. The hi-hat and ride cymbals are often used to create a flowing, triplet feel known as *swing*. Swing is an essential ingredient in many forms of popular music. In lesson 15 you will learn to play jazz styles with swing. For now, aim for a light, crisp cymbal sound over a steady beat.

Exercise 1:

Count aloud as you try these three simple triplet variations.

Swing notation

Rather than writing out swing parts with triplets, many musicians simply use quavers and mark the piece 'Swing' at the top. Compare the following examples.

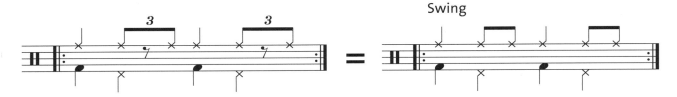

Exercise 2:

Now try these, building up the shuffle with a nice smooth 'swing' on the hi-hat. When you're happy with the way it feels, you could transfer over to the ride cymbal.

(a)
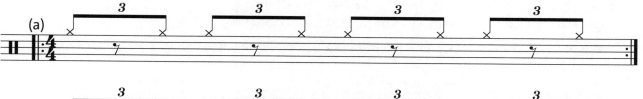

(b)
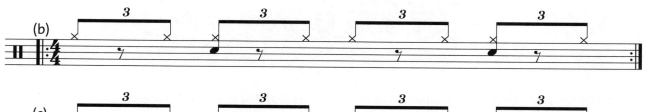

(c)
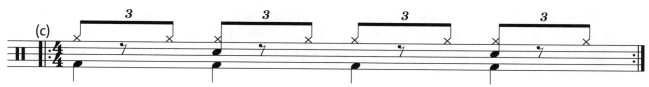

Half-time feel

If the standard snare backbeat on 2 and 4 (**a**) is replaced with a single snare note on beat 3 (**b**), the rhythm feels twice as slow as it really is.

This concept can be applied to most popular drumming styles.

Compare these two examples:

Blues Shuffle

(a)
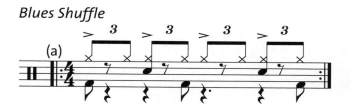

Blues Shuffle (half-time feel)

(b)

Exercise 3: variations

Here are some great variations on the basic shuffle. Don't forget to build the patterns up slowly as described on page 38.

Chicago Shuffle

(a)
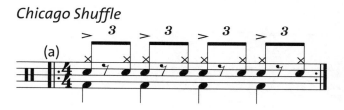

Texas Shuffle

(b)
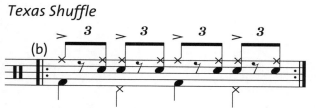

The final variation (d) is in half-time feel: look at the way the bass and snare are placed, and listen to the CD.

Swing Shuffle

(c)

Half-time Shuffle

(d)
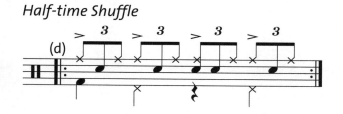

Lesson 10

Pick-ups

Often, drummers will play an introductory phrase, known as a *pick-up*.

Try either of these examples as a pick-up to any pattern from this lesson.

Now go back to lesson 9 and invent a pick-up for the basic rock rhythm.

Soon you will have your own list of pick-ups and fills that you can use to customise your drum parts.

In the next piece, notice the extra tom-tom notes and a crash cymbal on the last quaver of bar 5.

For the first time, bar numbers and *rehearsal marks* are included to help you keep track of where you are in the music. Feel free to add your own fills and other variations as you like!

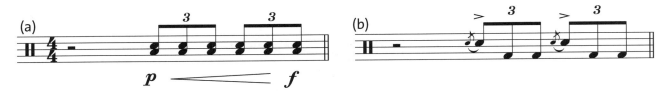

Pieces for Lesson 10

On The South Side

Pete Kershaw and Steve Kershaw

Berners St. Blues

Si Potts

27-28

♩ = 100 Swing (♪♪ = ♪³♪)

(straight)

1. Rudiments

(10)

Play the following rudiments:

- Five-Stroke Roll
- Buzz Roll
- Drag

2. Notation

(10)

Write out the following figures in full:

3. Pedal Power

(10)

See how quickly you can play the following piece (accurately!):

4. Research

(10)

Find the names of drummers from the following bands:

- Led Zeppelin
- Queen
- Metallica
- The Beatles
- Red Hot Chili Peppers
- The Police
- Jazz Messengers
- The Crusaders
- Cream
- Keith Jarrett Standards Trio

5. Terms

(10)

Write the meanings of these musical terms:

- Andante ....
- Crescendo ....

- Piano ....
- Sforzando ....

- Presto ....

Total (50)

1. **Reggae and ska drumming**
2. **Cross-stick**

3. **Rim shot**
4. **D.S. al Coda**

Reggae drumming

Reggae developed in Jamaica in the 1960s, growing out of Ska (see page 44). In reggae, the bass drum and bass guitar often emphasise beat 3 together: this is known as *one drop*. The rhythm guitar may play on the off-beat (2 and 4), creating a kind of backbeat. In reggae, this backbeat is known as the *skank*. Great reggae artists include Bob Marley, Black Uhuru and British band Steel Pulse.

The sound balance in reggae has a strong bass drum (the *one-drop*), with muffled tom-toms and a *cross-stick* snare (see below).

Photo courtesy of Ebet Roberts/Redferns

Sly Dunbar – working with bassist Robbie Shakespeare, together they became the most influential rhythm section in reggae. They built on the one-drop *style (see page 44) in the 1970s, emerging with several important new reggae styles.*

Cross-stick

The cross-stick is generally performed on the snare drum by turning over the drumstick.

With the butt end furthest away from the body, the tip of the stick is placed on the head.

The butt end is then struck on the drum rim, creating a short, dry metallic sound.

Cross-sticks are notated as a circled note on the snare drum line:

Rim shot

The rim shot is played on the snare drum by striking the drum head and rim at the same time. The result is a loud 'crack' sound.

Rim shots are notated as a circled x on the snare drum line: ⊗

Exercise 1:

Build up this one-drop pattern, part-by-part:

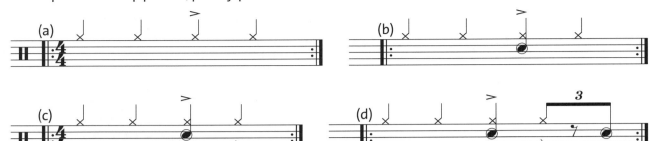

Exercise 2:

Now try these variations. Firstly, with swing triplet figures just like the ones in lesson 10 (**a**); and then with a bass drum on every beat (**b**), which is known as *four-on-the-floor*:

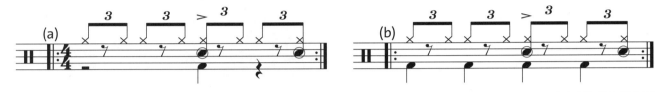

Ska drumming

The ska style brings together calypso and rhythm & blues elements, and is the foundation of reggae.
Ska rhythms can be very similar to those used in reggae, but often use four-on-the-floor bass drum and an off-beat hi-hat pattern. Ska is also often played at a faster tempo than reggae.

Exercise 3: preliminary exercise

Count out loud as you play these. Make sure that the off-beat hi-hat notes are crisp and accurate:

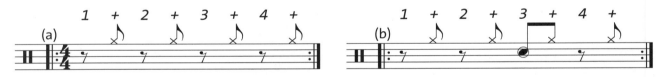

Exercise 4: ska variations

Listen to the examples on the CD and try them for yourself. Hear how these patterns are used in music by people like Prince Buster, Toots and the Maytals, and British group The Specials.

In the final variation (**e**) the hi-hat is played open on the last quaver of the pattern.

Experiment with the size of the gap between the hi-hat cymbals until you are happy with the sound.

D.S. AL CODA

Notice the *D.S. al Coda* in this piece.

D.S. is short for the Italian *Dal Segno*, meaning 'from the sign'.
Return to the sign 𝄋 , and play from there until the *Coda* symbol ⊕.
Continue on to the *Coda* section, marked again by ⊕.

In the piece for this lesson, various elements of reggae and ska are used. Notice especially the triplet groups: sometimes the middle one is missing, and other times it's the only one played.

Count out loud as you listen to the CD, and then try clapping along, before finally playing the part on your kit.

Piece for Lesson 11

Swing Low, Sweet Chariot

African-American Spiritual

33-34

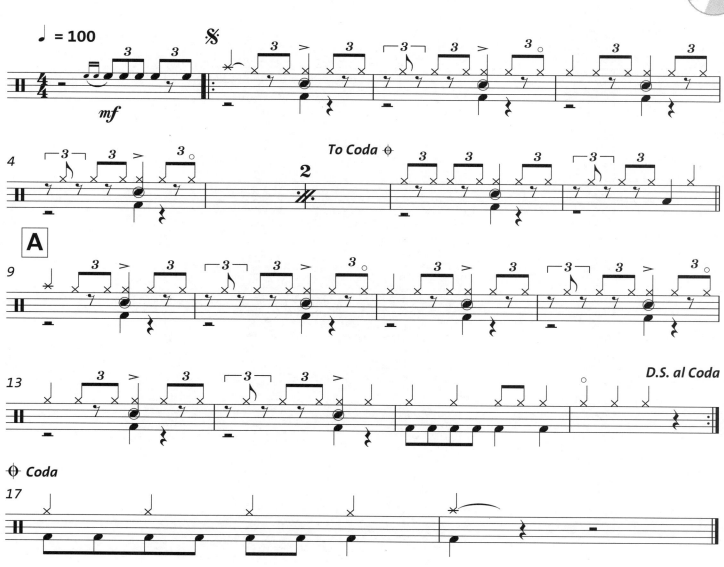

Piece for Lesson 11

Oh! Susanna

American traditional

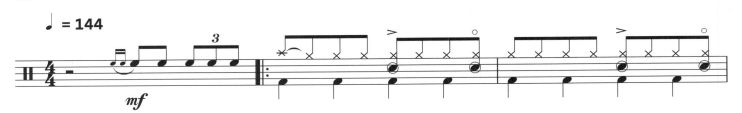

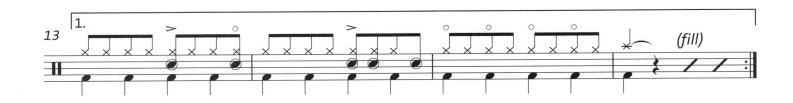

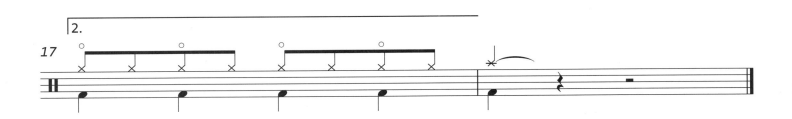

goals:

1. **Country drumming**
2. **Waltz**
3. **Pause sign**

Country drumming

Country is an American folk music style that has evolved through a combination of European folk music, blues, Southern church music and popular songs.

Country drumming incorporates many elements of both rock and blues, typically with a cross-stick on beats 2 and 4. The bass drum is most prominent, with the cross stick below this, and the hi-hat acts as a filler that 'ticks' over quietly in-between.

Photo courtesy of Lissa Wales/www.drumpics.com

Larrie Londin – his strong back-beat style characterised a career including work with such diverse talents as Elvis Presley, Merle Haggard, Dolly Parton and Chet Atkins.

37

Exercise 1:

Here are a number of different country-style patterns. Listen to the CD, and also listen to recordings by different people in these styles. Try your own variations. For instance you could use a cross-stick, or occasionally a rim shot, instead of a snare drum.

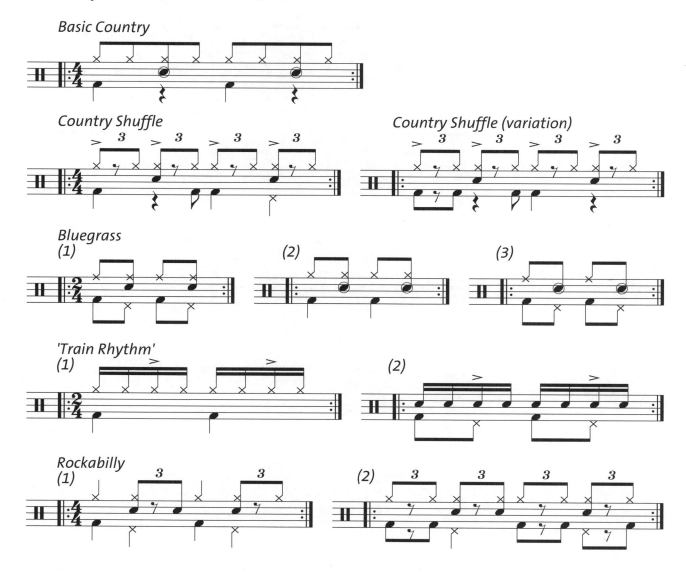

Basic Country

Country Shuffle

Country Shuffle (variation)

Bluegrass
(1)   *(2)*   *(3)*

'Train Rhythm'
(1)   *(2)*

Rockabilly
(1)   *(2)*

Waltz

The waltz is a dance style in $\frac{3}{4}$. The country waltz often uses the classic *boom chick-chick* sound (see fig. 2) in bass drum and hi-hat. Don't forget to work out your own $\frac{3}{4}$ fills, too!

Exercise 2: Waltz patterns

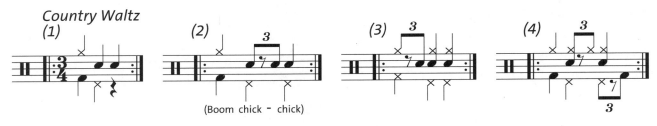

(Boom chick - chick)

Pause sign

The pause sign ⌢ indicates that the note(s) to which it is attached are held for longer than usual. It can be used to indicate a pause during a passage of music, or simply to show that the final note should be held on.

Piece for Lesson 12

Will The Circle Be Unbroken

Charles H. Gabriel

Pieces for Lesson 12

We Three Kings

Traditional

♩ = **100** *Swing* (♫ = ♩ ♪)

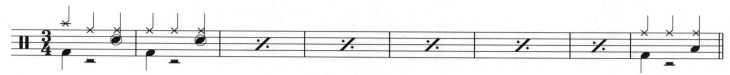

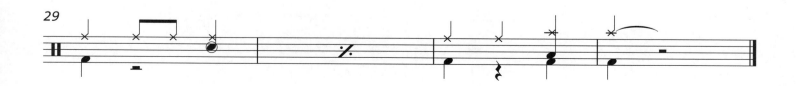

goals:

1. **Funk drumming**
2. **Syncopation**
3. **Ghost notes**
4. **Linear drumming**
5. **Substitution**

Photo courtesy of Andrew Lepley/Redferns

Steve Gadd – a hugely successful drummer known for his work with Paul Simon, James Taylor and Eric Clapton as well as jazz and funk recordings with many of America's greatest musicians. Gadd has a reputation for his ability to play 'in the pocket': creating a groove that locks into the other members of the rhythm section, whatever the style of music.

Funk drumming

Funk is an American style that brings together elements of rhythm & blues, soul and jazz. Typically funk uses complex rhythmic figures within very simple song structures. In funk, the bass guitar and bass drum often lock in to each other.

The bass drum is the most prominent in funk, with the snare drum behind, and light hi-hat notes added. 'Ghosted' snare drum beats are added as filler within a framework of semiquavers (sixteenth notes).

Syncopation

Stressing a note that would not normally be emphasised within a rhythmic pattern creates *syncopation*. Syncopation can be created by missing out expected notes on a strong beat, but syncopated notes can simply be those played just before or after a main beat, or in any unexpected place in the pattern. Syncopation is an important feature of funk music. Listen to Clyde Stubblefield's work for excellent examples of this.

Exercise 1:

Here's a basic rock pattern (**a**), followed by another (**b**) with extra bass drum notes, including a syncopated one on the 2nd quaver of beat 3 rather than straight on beat 3.

Ghost notes

Ghost notes are barely played at all. They create a subtle texture behind the main notes in a pattern. Ghost notes are shown in brackets.

Exercise 2:

Here's that same basic rock pattern again (**a**), followed this time (**b**) by a pattern containing a number of *ghosted* snare drum notes.

Linear drumming

In most kit drumming, a repeating pattern is set up on the cymbals, and the rhythm pattern is played on the rest of the kit against this. Up till now, almost every pattern you have played has had a regular cymbal part in the background. This generally means that bass, tom-tom and snare notes are played simultaneously with a cymbal note. In *linear* drumming, each drum is played in turn, the cymbals treated just like individual drums.

Exercise 3:

This time a variation on the familiar rock pattern (**a**) is followed by a linear version (**b**).
In the linear pattern, only one drum/cymbal is played at a time.

Substitution

By swapping a regularly-occurring sound with a less expected one, drummers create textures that can enhance syncopation. Swapping in this way is known as *substitution*.

Exercise 4:

Here are two substitutions for the rock pattern from exercise 3. Firstly (**a**), a tambourine is played on the first beat instead of the hi-hat (shown here with a diamond note-head ♩); and in the 2nd example (**b**), high and low (floor) tom-toms are also introduced:

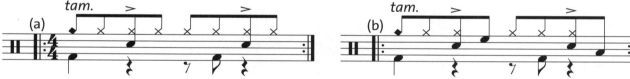 

The following piece features various elements from this lesson. Different funk rhythms are used, including a linear pattern in bars 18-24 and, from bars 26-32, a classic *disco* pattern with open hi-hats on the off-beats, a simple snare backbeat, and four-on-the-floor on the bass drum.

Notice also that one-bar repeat and two-bar repeat symbols are used. Where the original bar includes a crash cymbal at the beginning, which isn't required in the repeated bar, 'no crash' is written.

REPERTOIRE

Learning new styles and rhythms will help make you a flexible and versatile drummer.

Take the time to work out new rhythms you hear, and write them down for yourself.

Along with pick-ups, fills and other ornaments, you will have a growing collection
of personal favourites to use for different occasions.

Piece for Lesson 13

Abide With Me

Monk

goals:

1. **Latin American drumming**
2. **Bossa Nova**
3. **Samba**

Latin American drumming

Music from Latin America includes *Tango*, *Bossa Nova*, *Rumba*, *Samba* and *Salsa*.

Many Latin American styles are characterised by complex, syncopated rhythms, many of which present unique challenges to the drummer.

Bossa Nova

Bossa nova grew out of samba, and emerged in Brazil in the late 1950s.

One key sound in the bossa nova is the *clave* rhythm: the claves are a pair of hard-wood sticks playing a constant repeating pattern.

Photo courtesy of LFI

Desi Arnaz – an important Afro-Cuban percussionist. The conga is a leading Latin percussion instrument, and the principal instrument in the Rumba.

Photo courtesy of Latin Percussion

On the drum kit this is generally played with a cross-stick.

The clave rhythm is a two-bar phrase containing five notes, which can also be played with the bars swapped around. The rhythm is known as 3:2 when the first bar contains three notes; and as 2:3 when the three notes appear in the second bar.

This rhythm is known as the *son clave*:

A variation on the clave rhythm is the *rhumba clave*. It is a syncopated variation of the *son clave*.

Exercise 1: Bossa nova rhythm

Build up the bossa nova rhythm part-by-part, starting with the hi-hat (**a**), which should emulate the sound of a Brazilian shaker.

Then add the clave on cross-sticks (**b**). The regular, skipping bass drum is next (**c**).

In the final version (**d**), the hi-hat rhythm is moved to the ride cymbal, with a simple open-close rhythm added on the hi-hat pedal.

The overall effect should be light and airy. Listen to some bossa nova recordings to hear the authentic sound.

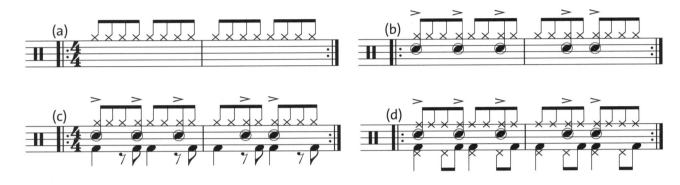

Samba

Samba has its roots in African dance and drumming, with Portuguese folk rhythms mixed in.

The samba is a very popular and energetic dance, in which the various parts of the rhythm pattern need to flow individually.

Exercise 2: Samba rhythm

Again, build up the rhythm one step at a time.

Begin with the hi-hat (**a**), and add the cross-stick part (**b**).

Once you've added the bass drum (**c**), and you are comfortable, switch the hi-hat part over to the ride cymbal (**d**), freeing the hi-hat up for off-beat pedal notes.

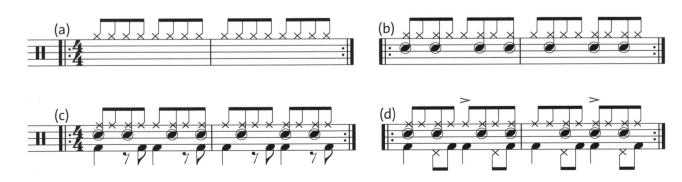

Piece for Lesson 14

Voodoo Girl

Pete Kershaw and Steve Kershaw

A

1. **Jazz drumming**
2. **Independence**

3. **Swing notation**
4. **Jazz phrasing**

Photo courtesy of LFI

Max Roach – one of the most important jazz drummers of all time, is especially known for his work with bebop *musicians such as Dizzy Gillespie and Charlie Parker. His fluid, inventive style elevated the role of the drums in jazz from rhythm instrument to extended solo contributor.*

Jazz drumming

Jazz is a melting pot of musical strands, with its roots in West African vocal styles, African American folk music (including blues), ragtime, European folk and military music, with dance rhythms and popular song forms mixed in.

Jazz is characterised by syncopation, swing, *poly-rhythms* (layering of different rhythms), call & response, and improvisation. Of all these elements, swing is perhaps the most important. In lesson 10, the triplet feel was introduced. Let's look a little more closely at the nature of swing.

Jazz patterns are generally based on a strong crotchet pulse with triplet embellishments. Emphasis is placed on the ride cymbal, often with the hi-hat played with the foot. These two instruments are played the loudest and can act as time-keepers for the band.

53

Exercise 1: jazz ride cymbal patterns

Depending on the tempo, the ride cymbal beat can be played in various ways.

Play a steady beat on the ride cymbal (**a**); if the beat is slow (**b**), the off-beat ride cymbal notes will be on the 3rd part of a triplet. At a fast tempo (**c**), the off-beat notes are played almost *straight* (without swing).

Now play the pattern at a medium tempo with bass drum added (**d**) and with heavy accents on each beat with the ride cymbal. Be sure to feel the rolling triplet pattern as swing: light and crisp.

Notice that the tempo of (c) is so fast that the beats are counted in minims, not crotchets.

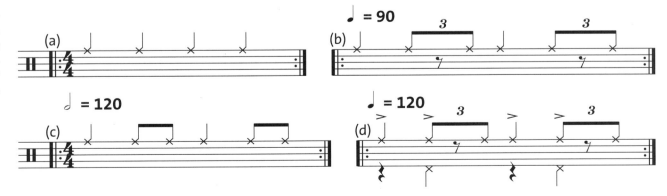

Independence

Many drummers enjoy the challenge of independence exercises, and in jazz drumming they are crucial to developing spontaneity. These exercises will improve your drumming regardless of the style of music you choose to pursue.

Exercise 2: independence exercises

Practise these as slowly as you need to at first, and part-by-part if necessary. They will be worth the effort!

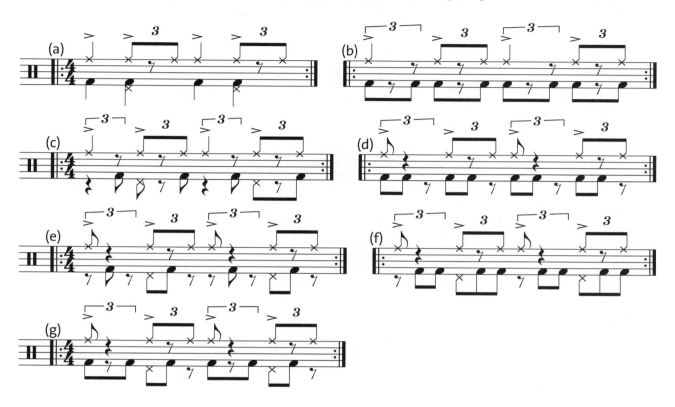

When you are comfortable with these rhythms, try adding snare-drum accents for variety.

BUILDING NEW PATTERNS

When learning new patterns, begin by playing the top line of cymbals and hi-hat, until that feels comfortable. Now work your way down the stave, adding each instrument in turn only when you are ready.

Start slowly at first, building up speed when you feel able.

If you find it difficult to write out new rhythms and fills using standard drum notation, try using the grid on page 63.

Fill in the squares on the correct beat for each drum, and then write the standard notation beneath.

Feel free to photocopy the page so you can use it again and again.

Exercise 3: Jazz styles

Finally, here are some common jazz patterns. Try them at various tempos and listen to as many jazz recordings as you can. You will soon learn to recognise different feels and even different drummers.

Collect your own favourite fills and try them out when playing with other musicians.

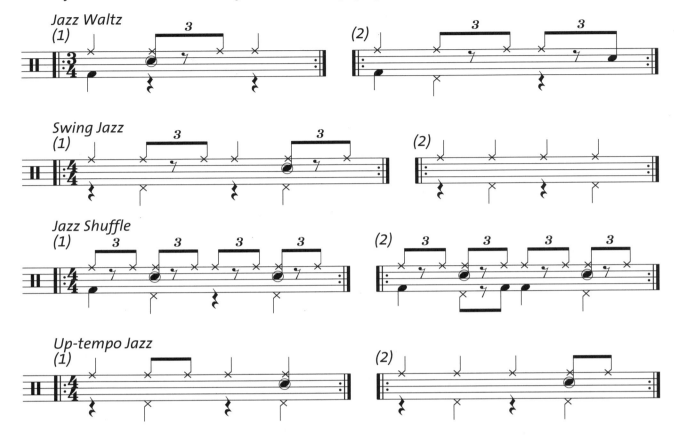

In the next piece, various different jazz patterns are given, together with a number of opportunities for fills. At letter E, you are asked to play *ad lib* – that is, improvising. Add your own embellishments and try different sounds.

Notice that a suggested rhythm is given for the fill in the repeated section near the end (bar 41). Use this as a guide only, but listen to the other instruments on the CD to help you decide exactly what to play.

Piece for Lesson 15

Kitsbury Strut

Pete Kershaw and Steve Kershaw

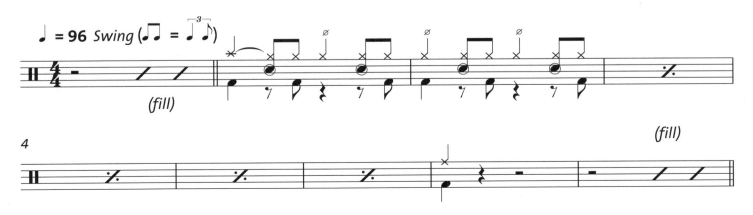

test: *for* Lessons 11 to 15

1. **Styles**

Play a sample pattern in the following styles:

(10)

- Funk
- Swing
- Country
- Ska
- Rock

2. **Test your reflexes**

Play this independence exercise:

(10)

3. **Tempos**

Beat out the following tempos, then check them with a metronome:

(10)

- 100 bpm
- 65 bpm
- 140 bpm

4. **Symbols**

What do these symbols mean?

(10)

⊗ ....

♩ ....

5. **Terms**

Write the meanings of these musical terms:

(10)

- D.S. al Coda ....

- Sim. ....

- Diminuendo ....

- Forte ....

Total (50)

- Adagio ....

Performance Pieces

Jingle Bells Rock

Traditional (arr. C. Baker)

58–59

Can-Can

Offenbach

Drum Maps

Use these grids to chart new rhythms, and to help you write them down using conventional notation underneath.

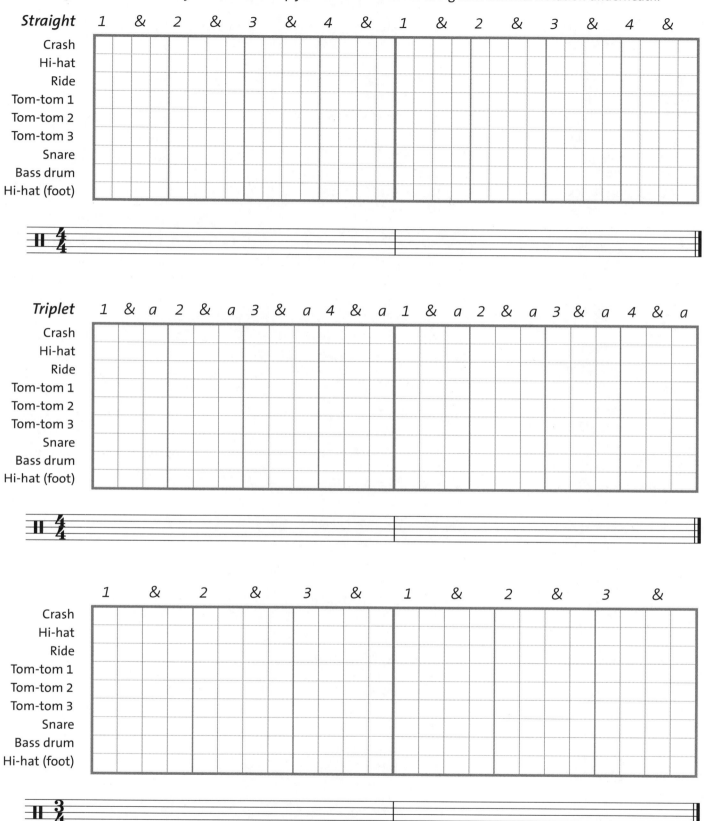

Photocopiable resource
This page is included to allow you to chart your drum rhythms and to make limited photocopies
solely for the purpose of private study, and not for commercial reproduction or sale.

CD backing tracks

1   Virtuoso Performance

2   Au Clair de la Lune *demonstration*

3   Au Clair de la Lune *backing only*

4   Twinkle Twinkle, Little Star *demonstration*

5   Twinkle Twinkle, Little Star *backing only*

6   Anitra's Dance *demonstration*

7   Anitra's Dance *backing only*

8   Early One Morning *demonstration*

9   Early One Morning *backing only*

10   The First Nowell *demonstration*

11   The First Nowell *backing only*

12   Lesson 6 Duet *demonstration*

13   Frère Jacques *demonstration*

14   Frère Jacques *backing only*

15   The Drunken Sailor *demonstration*

16   The Drunken Sailor *backing only*

17   Big Six *demonstration*

18   Jingle Bells *demonstration*

19   Jingle Bells *backing only*

20   Auld Lang Syne *demonstration*

21   Auld Lang Syne *backing only*

22   Lesson 10 Exercise 2 *demonstration*

23   Lesson 10 Half-time feel *demonstration*

24   Lesson 10 Exercise 3 *demonstration*

25   On The South Side *demonstration*

26   On The South Side *backing only*

27   Berners St. Blues *demonstration*

28   Berners St. Blues *backing only*

29   Lesson 11 Exercise 1 *demonstration*

30   Lesson 11 Exercise 2 *demonstration*

31   Lesson 11 Exercise 3 *demonstration*

32   Lesson 11 Exercise 4 *demonstration*

33   Swing Low, Sweet Chariot *demonstration*

34   Swing Low, Sweet Chariot *backing only*

35   Oh! Susanna *demonstration*

36   Oh! Susanna *backing only*

37   Lesson 12 Exercise 1 *demonstration*

38   Lesson 12 Exercise 2 *demonstration*

39   Will The Circle Be Unbroken *demonstration*

40   Will The Circle Be Unbroken *backing only*

41   We Three Kings *demonstration*

42   We Three Kings *backing only*

43   Lesson 13 Exercise 1 *demonstration*

44   Lesson 13 Exercise 2 *demonstration*

45   Lesson 13 Exercise 3 *demonstration*

46   Lesson 13 Exercise 4 *demonstration*

47   Abide With Me *demonstration*

48   Abide With Me *backing only*

49   Lesson 14 Exercise 1 *demonstration*

50   Lesson 14 Exercise 2 *demonstration*

51   Voodoo Girl *demonstration*

52   Voodoo Girl *backing only*

53   Lesson 15 Exercise 1 *demonstration*

54   Lesson 15 Exercise 2 *demonstration*

55   Lesson 15 Exercise 3 *demonstration*

56   Kitsbury Strut *demonstration*

57   Kitsbury Strut *backing only*

58   Jingle Bells Rock *demonstration*

59   Jingle Bells Rock *backing only*

60   Can-Can *demonstration*

61   Can-Can *backing only*

62   Practice track: 65 bpm

63   Practice track: 80 bpm

64   Practice track: 100 bpm

65   Practice track: 120 bpm

66   Practice track: 140 bpm

How to use the CD

After track 1, which gives an idea of how the drums can sound, the backing tracks are listed in the order in which they appear in the book

Look for the symbol in the book for the relevant demonstration or backing track

To remove the CD from the plastic sleeve, lift the small lip to break the perforations. Replace the disc after use for convenient storage.

1 2 3 4 5 6 7 8 9